PEOPLE

How to Use Your SD-X Reader with This Book

This highly interactive book lets you explore the world in an interactive format. You can read the book and study the maps, photographs, and illustrations, but a touch of the SD-X Reader adds in-depth audio information, word definitions, and learning games to the pictures and maps.

1. Press the Power button to turn the SD-X Reader on or off. The LED will light up when the SD-X Reader is on.

2. Touch the volume buttons found on this page or on the Table of Contents page to adjust the volume.

3. Touch photographs, maps, and illustrations with the SD-X Reader to hear additional information. In a block of text, touch words that are a different color or size to hear a definition or more information.

4. As you touch around the page, you'll encounter games and quizzes. Touch the header or image that started the game to stop playing the game.

5. After two minutes of inactivity, the Reader will beep and go to sleep.

6. If the batteries are low, the Reader will beep twice and the LED will start blinking. Replace the batteries by following the instructions on the next page. The SD-X Reader uses two AAA batteries.

7. To use headphones or earbuds, plug them into the headphone jack on the bottom of the SD-X Reader.

CHANGE THE VOLUME WITH THESE BUTTONS

UP   DOWN

Battery Information
Interactive Pen includes 2 replaceable AAA batteries (UM-4 or LR03).

Battery Installation
1. Open battery door with small flat-head or Phillips screwdriver.
2. Install new batteries according to +/- polarity. If batteries are not installed properly, the device will not function.
3. Replace battery door; secure with small screw.

Battery Safety
Batteries must be replaced by adults only. Properly dispose of used batteries. Do not dispose of batteries in fire; batteries may explode or leak. See battery manufacturer for disposal recommendations. Do not mix alkaline, standard (carbon-zinc), or rechargeable (nickel-cadmium) batteries. Do not mix old and new batteries. Only recommended batteries of the same or equivalent type should be used. Remove weakened or dead batteries. Never short-circuit the supply terminals. Non-rechargeable batteries are not to be recharged. Do not use rechargeable batteries. If batteries are swallowed, in the USA, promptly see a doctor and have the doctor phone 1-202-625-3333 collect. In other countries, have the doctor call your local poison control center. Batteries should be changed when sounds mix, distort, or become otherwise unintelligible as batteries weaken. The electrostatic discharge may interfere with the sound module. If this occurs, please simply restart the product.

In Europe, the dustbin symbol indicates that batteries, rechargeable batteries, button cells, battery packs, and similar materials must not be discarded in household waste. Batteries containing hazardous substances are harmful to the environment and to health. Please help to protect the environment from health risks by telling your children to dispose of batteries properly and by taking batteries to local collection points. Batteries handled in this manner are safely recycled.

Warning: Changes or modifications to this unit not expressly approved by the party responsible for compliance could void the user's authority to operate the equipment.

NOTE: This equipment has been tested and found to comply with the limits for a Class B digital device, pursuant to Part 15 of the FCC Rules. These limits are designed to provide reasonable protection against harmful interference in a residential installation. This equipment generates, uses, and can radiate radio frequency energy and, if not installed and used in accordance with the instructions, may cause harmful interference to radio communications. However, there is no guarantee that interference will not occur in a particular installation. If this equipment does cause harmful interference to radio or television reception, which can be determined by turning the equipment off and on, the user is encouraged to try to correct the interference by one or more of the following measures: Reorient or relocate the receiving antenna. Increase the separation between the equipment and receiver. Connect the equipment into an outlet on a circuit different from that to which the receiver is connected. Consult the dealer or an experienced radio TV technician for help.

Cover art from Shutterstock.com.

Interior art from Encyclopædia Britannica, Inc., Getty Images, Library of Congress, and Shutterstock.com. Page 56 and 57 art from NASA.

Louis Weber, CEO
Publications International, Ltd.
7373 North Cicero Avenue
Lincolnwood, Illinois 60712

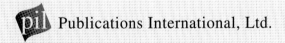

Customer Service
customer_service@pubint.com

ISBN: 978-1-4508-8409-9

Manufactured in China.

8 7 6 5 4 3 2 1

CONTENTS

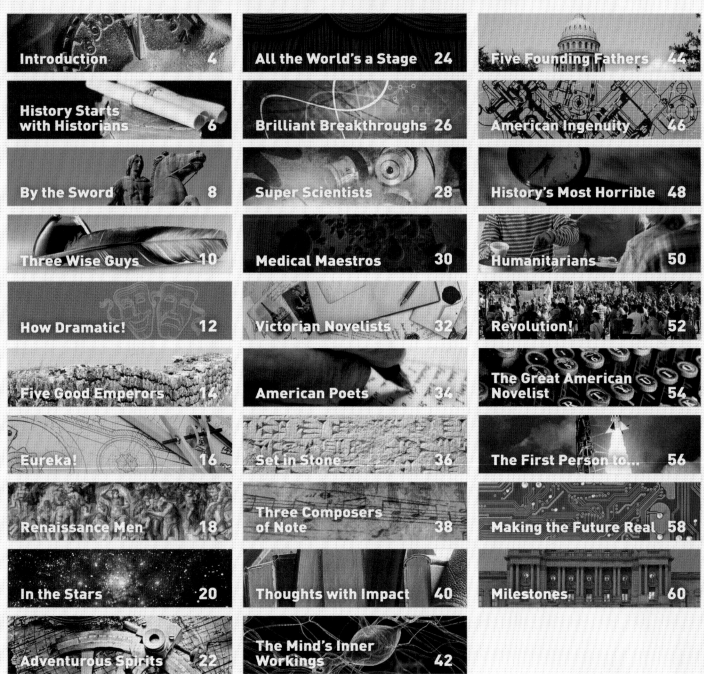

CHANGE THE VOLUME WITH THESE BUTTONS

UP   DOWN

INTRODUCTION

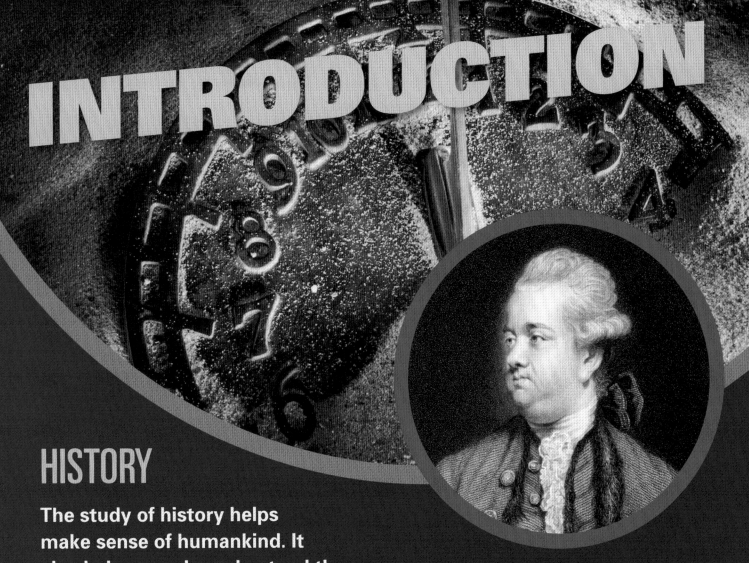

HISTORY

The study of history helps make sense of humankind. It also helps people understand the things that happen today and that may happen in the future.

EDWARD GIBBON (1737–94)
The Decline and Fall of the Roman Empire

ANNE FRANK (1929–45)
The Diary of a Young Girl

DIARY

A diary is a daily personal record. In it the writer is free to record anything at all. This may include events, comments, ideas, reading notes, or any subject on one's mind as the entry that covers the day is written.

JAMES BOSWELL (1740–95)
The Life of Samuel Johnson, LL.D.

BIOGRAPHY

History and biography have several similarities, but they are not the same. Both the biographer and the historian search for evidence. They evaluate the information they find to decide if it is factual and relevant. History, however, is the recorded past of human societies; it tells the story of nations, wars, movements—the whole range of past human activity. Biography deals with a single life story.

AUTOBIOGRAPHY

The life story of an individual, as written by himself, is called autobiography. It differs from biography in that the person presents himself to his readers as he views himself and as he wants to be understood by others.

BENJAMIN FRANKLIN (1706–90)
The Autobiography of Benjamin Franklin

HISTORY STARTS WITH HISTORIANS

A sense of the past is a light that illuminates the present and directs attention toward the possibilities of the future. Without an adequate knowledge of history, today's events are disconnected occurrences. History is a science—a branch of knowledge that uses specific methods and tools to achieve its goals. To compile a history, records are needed. Some of these are written records: government papers, diaries, letters, inscriptions, biographies, and many others.

HISTORICAL TERMS

biography

legend

myth

historiography

history

WHAT A HISTORIAN DOES

YES | NO

GREEK ACHIEVEMENT

The first historian of any significance in Greece was Hecataeus of Miletus, a native of Asia Minor who lived in the 6th and 5th centuries BC. Only fragments of his *History* and *Tour Around the World* have survived. He looked critically at the Greeks' attempts to account for their past and concluded: "The stories of the Greeks are numerous and in my opinion ridiculous."

Greek historians, especially Herodotus and Thucydides, made at least two significant contributions to the writing of history. They weighed the evidence, attempting to separate the true from the false or fanciful. They also wrote about the recent past. Herodotus dealt with the Persian Wars in his *History*. Thucydides wrote a history of the Peloponnesian War, an event through which he lived. He says of his research: "With reference to the narrative of events, far from permitting myself to derive it from the first source that came to hand, I did not even trust my own impressions, but it rests partly on what I saw myself, partly on what others saw for me, the accuracy of the report always being tried by the most severe and detailed tests possible."

HERODOTUS (484?–425? BC)

Herodotus was the author of the first great narrative history produced in the ancient world, the *History* of the Greco-Persian Wars.

THUCYDIDES (460?–404? BC)

The greatest of ancient Greek historians, Thucydides wrote the *History of the Peloponnesian War*, which recounts the struggle between Athens and Sparta in the 5th century BC. His work was the first recorded political and moral analysis of a nation's war policies.

XENOPHON (430?–355? BC)

Xenophon wrote of the military campaigns in which he served as a young officer. His best-known book, *Anabasis* ("Upcountry March"), tells of the march and retreat of the Greek auxiliary army in the service of the Persian prince Cyrus. Xenophon also wrote a memorial to the life of Socrates.

BY THE SWORD

ALEXANDER THE GREAT
(356–323 BC)

As a general Alexander is among the greatest the world has known. He showed unusual versatility both in the combination of different arms and in adapting his tactics to the challenge of enemies who commanded novel forms of warfare—the Śaka nomads, the Indian hill tribes, or Porus with his elephants. Alexander's strategy was skillful and imaginative, and he knew how to exploit the chances that arise in every battle and may be decisive for victory or defeat; he also drew the last advantage from victory by relentless pursuit. Alexander's use of cavalry was so effective that he rarely had to fall back upon his infantry to deliver the crushing blow.

THE EMPIRE OF
ALEXANDER THE GREAT
— ALEXANDER'S ROUTE
☐ ALEXANDER'S EMPIRE
☒ BATTLE

JULIUS CAESAR (100?–44 BC)

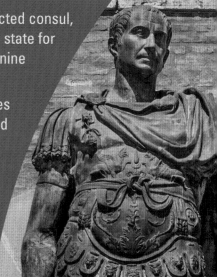

Julius Caesar studied public speaking and later entered politics. In 59 BC he was elected consul, the highest public office in ancient Rome. As one of two consuls, he ruled the Roman state for one year. He then left Rome to govern a Roman province in Gaul (modern France). In nine years of fighting he brought all of Gaul under Roman rule.

Caesar made himself dictator in 49 BC. Five years of civil war between Caesar's forces and the supporters of the popular general Pompey followed. Pompey fled to Egypt and died there before Caesar could catch him.

Many Romans wanted to be a republic governed by a group of people rather than a dictatorship led by one man alone. Sixty senators agreed to a plan to kill Caesar on March 15 (the "Ides of March" in the Roman calendar), 44 BC. Among them was Caesar's friend Marcus Junius Brutus. As he died, Caesar said, "Et tu, Brute?" ("You too, Brutus?").

HANNIBAL (247–183? BC)

One of the greatest military leaders of ancient times, Hannibal was a general of Carthage, a city in North Africa. He led the Carthaginian forces against Rome in the Second Punic War. This war began after he attacked Saguntum, a city in eastern Spain. Soon Hannibal decided to take the war into Italy. While the Romans made plans to invade Carthage, Hannibal started moving toward Rome. It became one of history's most daring marches. He led his forces through eastern Spain, over the Pyrenees Mountains, and across the Rhône River in what is now southern France.

Only about half of Hannibal's forces reached northern Italy. Nevertheless, they defeated the Romans several times. In 216 BC Hannibal and his troops crushed the Romans near the village of Cannae, in southeastern Italy. In this battle the Carthaginians killed some 60,000 Roman soldiers. Hannibal was never able to win another battle as great as the one at Cannae.

SCIPIO AFRICANUS (236–183? BC)

In 210 BC Scipio Africanus accepted the generalship of the army in Spain. He then conquered New Carthage (now Cartagena, Spain). By 206 he had defeated all the armies of Carthage in Spain and given Rome control of the province. Next he set out to defeat Carthage's home base in Africa. He landed there with about 35,000 men in 204. By 202, with the great battle of Zama, Scipio had defeated Carthage completely.

IF YOU WERE ON AN ANCIENT BATTLEFIELD...

cavalry   legion   phalanx   hoplite   trireme

TRUE OR FALSE?

T F

THREE WISE GUYS

SOCRATES (470?–399 BC)

Socrates shunned the shallow notion of truth for its own sake. He turned to his conscience for moral truth and enjoyed creating confusion by asking simple questions. He sought to uncover the nature of virtue and to find a rule of life. Favorite objects of his attacks were the Sophists, who charged a fee for their teaching. "Know thyself" was the motto he is reputed to have learned from the oracle at Delphi. In knowing oneself he saw the possibility of learning what is really good, in contrast to accepting mere outward appearance.

SOCRATES' DEATH

Socrates was not always appreciated by the Athenian population. His genius for exposing pompous frauds made him many enemies. At last, three of his political foes indicted him on the charge of "neglect of the gods" and "corruption of the young." They were false charges, but politically convenient. He was sentenced to die by drinking hemlock.

DID YOU KNOW?

Socrates did not wear shoes. He always went about barefoot, even in winter.

PLATO (428?–348? BC)

The influence of Plato has been persistent and unbroken. His Academy at Athens was opened in about 387 BC. It was a school devoted to philosophy, law, and scientific research—primarily mathematics—and it endured as an institution until AD 529.

PLATO'S ACADEMY

Plato's Academy was the ultimate ancestor of the modern university. It was an influential center of research and learning, attracting many men of outstanding ability. The great mathematicians Theaetetus (417–369 BC) and Eudoxus of Cnidus (c. 395–c. 342 BC) were associated with it. Although Plato was not a research mathematician, he was aware of the results of those who were, and he made use of them in his own work. For 20 years Aristotle was also a member of the Academy. He started his own school, the Lyceum, after Plato's death.

WHO SAID IT?

ARISTOTLE (384–322 BC)

Aristotle laid the foundation for most modern sciences. He thought that people should observe nature and gain knowledge from their senses. He argued that any theory must be based on observed facts. No one bettered Aristotle's work on logic or zoology for about 2,000 years.

DID YOU KNOW?

Aristotle was Alexander the Great's teacher.

ARISTOTLE'S PERIPATETIC SCHOOL

At his school in Athens, Aristotle taught brilliantly, collected the first great library, and established a museum. Because he walked about while teaching, Athenians called his school the Peripatetic (which means "to walk about") school. He led his pupils in research in every existing field of knowledge. They dissected animals and studied the habits of insects. The science of observation was new to the Greeks. Hampered by lack of instruments, they were not always correct in their conclusions.

One of Aristotle's most important contributions was defining and classifying the various branches of knowledge. He sorted them into physics, metaphysics, psychology, rhetoric, poetics, and logic and thus laid the foundation of most of the sciences of today.

HOW DRAMATIC!

Scholars believe that drama dates back to the time of the earliest peoples. Drama probably began as part of religious festivals and ceremonies. These took place in many cultures, including those of ancient Egypt, India, and China.

Western drama has its roots in ancient Greece. The great age of Greek drama was the 400s BC. Greek drama was written in poetry. A few actors portrayed all the play's characters. Greek playwrights also wrote parts for a group called the chorus. The chorus stood off to the side and described and explained the action. Greek tragedies told about important people and events from legends or history. The comedies from this period often made fun of the day's political figures.

SOPHOCLES:
SEVEN SURVIVING PLAYS

ELECTRA   AJAX   ANTIGONE

OEDIPUS REX   PHILOCTETES

TRACHINIAN WOMEN

OEDIPUS AT COLONUS

SOPHOCLES (496?–406 BC)

Sophocles was a master of tragic drama, especially in his characterizations. His tragic women are probably his most outstanding characters—Electra, Antigone, Deianeira, and others. He also had great ability to devise well-constructed plots. He has been criticized, however, for not dealing forcefully with the political issues of the time, as Euripides did, or with religious themes that were explored by Aeschylus.

AESCHYLUS (525–456 BC)

Aeschylus is said to have introduced into Greek drama the second actor. This not only was an exciting break from the traditional single performer and chorus but also allowed for a variety of plots and dialogue. Aeschylus reduced the size and the role of the chorus. He used some unusual scenic effects as well as exotic and often terrifying masks and costumes. He probably acted in most of his own plays, which was the usual practice among dramatists of his time.

THE PLAYS OF AESCHYLUS

Out of more than 80 known titles, 52 of his plays won first prizes. Only seven of the tragedies survive: the trilogy *Oresteia*, which includes *Agamemnon*, *Choephoroi*, and *Eumenides*; *The Suppliants*; *The Persians*; S*even Against Thebes*; and *Prometheus*.

EURIPIDES (484?–406 BC)

Euripides invented protagonists quite different from the larger-than-life characters drawn with such conviction by Aeschylus and Sophocles. They were, for the most part, commonplace, down-to-earth men and women who had all the flaws and vulnerabilities ordinarily associated with human beings.

Euripides differed from Aeschylus and Sophocles in making his characters' tragic fates stem almost entirely from their own flawed natures and uncontrolled passions. Chance, disorder, and human irrationality and immorality frequently result not in an eventual reconciliation or moral resolution but in apparently meaningless suffering that is looked upon with indifference by the gods.

THEATRICAL WORDS

- epic
- tragedy
- act
- chorus
- prologue

THE ORIGINAL ROMANTIC COMEDY?

During the last decade of his career Euripides began to write "tragedies" that might actually be called romantic dramas, or tragicomedies with happy endings. These plays have a highly organized structure leading to a recognition scene in which the discovery of a character's true identity produces a complete change in the situation, and in general a happy one.

THE HOMERIC LEGEND

The individual who has traditionally been credited with putting the great epic poems the *Iliad* and the *Odyssey* into writing is Homer. Little else, however, is known of his life. The two epics provided the basis of Greek education and culture throughout the Classical age and formed the backbone of humane education down to the time of the Roman Empire and the spread of Christianity.

FIVE GOOD EMPERORS

The ancient Roman imperial succession of Nerva (reigned AD 96–98), Trajan (98–117), Hadrian (117–138), Antoninus Pius (138–161), and Marcus Aurelius (161–180) presided over the most majestic days of the Roman Empire. The period witnessed considerable expansion of the empire, from northern Britain to Dacia and to Arabia and Mesopotamia. The empire was consolidated, its defenses were perfected, and a tolerably uniform provincial system covered the whole area of the empire. Historians for many years viewed this period as a high point of human history.

IMPERIAL ATTRIBUTES

HADRIAN'S WALL took six years to build, and it was expanded in later years. It was at least 12 feet (about 3.7 meters) high in the eastern section

NERVA

The keynote of Nerva's regime was a skillfully propagandized renunciation of the terrorist means by which the previous emperor had imposed his tyranny.

TRAJAN

Trajan was a much more active ruler than Nerva had been during his short reign. Instead of returning to Rome at once to become emperor, he remained either to make preparations for a coming campaign into Dacia or to ensure that discipline was restored and defenses strengthened. He behaved with respect and affability toward the Senate. He was generous to the populace of Rome, to whom he distributed considerable cash gifts, and increased the number of poor citizens who received free grain from the state.

HADRIAN

Hadrian regarded his 20-year reign as a golden age of peace and prosperity, comparable to that of his great predecessor Augustus more than 100 years earlier. Monuments to Hadrian's reign are the Tivoli villa near Rome, Italy; Castel Sant'Angelo, adjacent to Vatican City, built as a mausoleum for himself; the Pantheon, a temple to the gods, in Rome; and Hadrian's Wall in the north of England.

ANTONINUS PIUS

References to Antoninus in 2nd-century literature are exceptionally scanty; it is certain that few striking events occurred during his 23-year reign. The feeling of well-being that pervaded the empire under Antoninus is reflected in the celebrated praise by the orator Aelius Aristides in 143–144. After Antoninus's death, however, the empire suffered invasion by hostile tribes, followed by severe civil strife.

MARCUS AURELIUS

A great task faced Marcus Aurelius when he became Roman emperor in AD 161. Generations of luxury had made the patricians weak and selfish. The middle class was disappearing, and the working class was being reduced to a state of slavery. Germanic tribes were at the borders of the empire.

Although Marcus loved peace, he was a good warrior and succeeded in defending the border provinces against invasion. In his spare moments he jotted down the rules that guided his own conduct. The resulting volume of *Meditations* was for many generations one of the world's most admired books of practical and political wisdom.

EUREKA!

The Latin word *scientia*, which means "knowing" or "being skilled," is the source of the English word *science*. No science is ever a fixed body of knowledge. This is indicated by the word *scientific*, which means science making—an ongoing process of searching for new information. When the process of making knowledge ceases, what is left is a tradition to be passed from one generation to another. Science does not exclude its tradition but continues developing it. In a letter to physicist Robert Hooke, Isaac Newton paid tribute to science makers who preceded him: "If I have seen further than you or Descartes it is by standing on the shoulders of giants."

LEONARDO DA VINCI

Birthplace: Florence, Italy

Born: 1452

Died: 1519

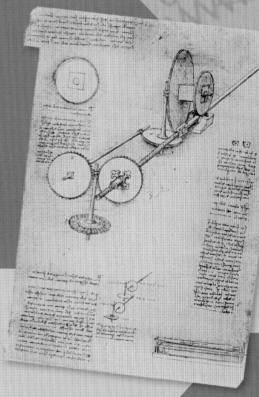

A page from one of Leonardo da Vinci's notebooks shows the operation of a mechanical wing.

THREE ANCIENT INNOVATORS

ARCHIMEDES (290/280–212/211 BC)

EUCLID (born c. 300 BC)

ERATOSTHENES (276?–194? BC)

AN INGENIOUS INVENTION

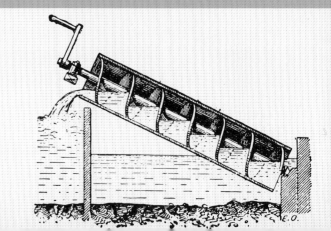

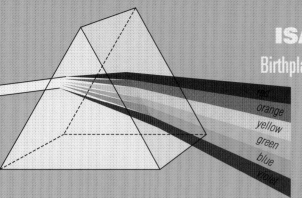

ISAAC NEWTON

Birthplace: Woolsthorpe, England

Born: 1642

Died: 1727

Newton's experiments with light showed that white light passed through a prism broke up into a wide color band, called a spectrum.

NOTABLE FIRSTS

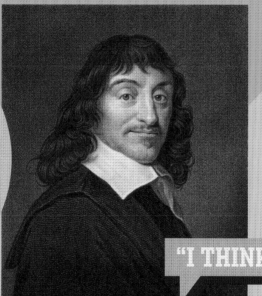

RENÉ DESCARTES

Birthplace: La Haye, France

Born: 1596

Died: 1650

"I THINK, THEREFORE I AM."

GOTTFRIED WILHELM LEIBNIZ

Birthplace: Leipzig, Germany

Born: 1646

Died: 1716

LEIBNIZ: UNIVERSAL GENIUS

- perfected the calculating machine
- laid the ground for integral and differential calculus
- founded dynamics, an area of mechanics
- worked on mechanical devices such as clocks, hydraulic presses, lamps, submarines, and windmills
- perfected the binary system of numeration used today in computer operations
- devised the theory that all reasoning can be reduced to an ordered combination of elements such as numbers, words, sounds, or colors (the theoretical basis of modern computers)
- laid the foundation for general topology, a branch of mathematics

RENAISSANCE MEN

The modern period of history is often considered to have begun with the Renaissance, one of the rare periods of genius in the world's history. The Renaissance began in Italy during the 14th century and reached its height in the 15th century before spreading throughout the rest of Europe.

After centuries of stiff symbolic representation, artists began again to study nature itself and to work from the living model. New ideas of grace, harmony, and beauty were gained from the sculpture and other artistic remains of classical Greece and Rome.

ARTISTIC ACHIEVEMENTS

THE SISTINE CHAPEL FRESCOES

MICHELANGELO
(1475–1564)

DAVID

MADONNA OF THE HARPIES

ANDREA del SARTO (1486–1530)

SAINT MARK

DONATELLO (1386?–1466)

MADONNA OF THE MEADOWS

RAPHAEL (1483–1520)

THE DESCENT OF THE HOLY GHOST

TITIAN (1488/90?–1576)

IN THE STARS

Since the beginnings of humankind people have gazed at the heavens. Before the dawn of history someone noticed that certain celestial bodies moved in orderly and predictable paths, and astronomy—an ancient science—was born.

PTOLEMY:
ANCIENT ASTRONOMER

GALILEO GALILEI

Birthplace: Pisa, Italy

Born: 1564

Died: 1642

Galileo's great contribution to scientific thinking was the principle of inertia. Before his time everyone followed Aristotle's theory that when an object moved, something had to act continuously to keep it moving. Galileo countered this with the theory that if a body is moving freely, something must happen to stop it or to make it change direction.

NICOLAUS COPERNICUS

Birthplace: Torun, Poland

Born: 1473

Died: 1543

Polish astronomer Nicolaus Copernicus is often considered the founder of modern astronomy. His study led to his theory that Earth and the other planets revolve around the Sun.

JOHANNES KEPLER

Birthplace: Weil der Stadt, Germany

Born: 1571

Died: 1630

KEPLER'S LAWS

1 The path of every planet in its motion about the Sun forms an ellipse, with the Sun at one focus.

2 The speed of a planet in its orbit varies so that a line joining it with the Sun sweeps over equal areas in equal times.

3 The squares of the planets' periods of revolution are proportional to the cubes of the planets' mean distances from the Sun.

NAME THAT ASTRONOMER

TYCHO BRAHE

Birthplace: Scania region of Denmark

Born: 1546

Died: 1601

In 1563, when Tycho Brahe made his first recorded observation of an alignment of Jupiter and Saturn, he found that the existing records of the positions of stars and planets were grossly inaccurate. The Copernican tables were several days off in predicting this event. In his youthful enthusiasm Tycho decided to devote his life to accumulating accurate observations of the heavens in order to correct the existing tables.

ADVENTUROUS SPIRITS

In the 1400s and 1500s European explorers undertook numerous long-distance sea voyages, initially in search of new trade routes. Their search brought them into contact with peoples and lands that were new to them. Voyages of exploration, or "discovery," shaped European politics and culture. However, the term "discovery" is placed in quotation marks because indigenous peoples had already explored their own lands.

CHRISTOPHER COLUMBUS

Birthplace: Genoa, Italy
Born: 1451
Died: 1506

Columbus landed in the New World by accident. He was seeking a western sea route from Europe to Asia. When he sighted land, he believed that he had reached his goal. And to the day he died he still believed that he had reached Asia.

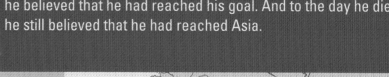

VASCO de GAMA

Birthplace: Sines, Portugal
Born: 1460?
Died: 1524

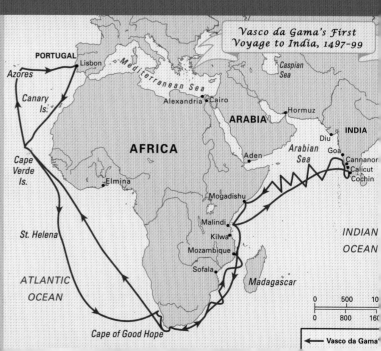

Vasco da Gama's First Voyage to India, 1497-99

SIR FRANCIS DRAKE

Birthplace: Devonshire, England

Born: 1543?

Died: 1596

Drake died on board his ship in January 1596 off the coast of Panama. More than any other of England's bold privateers, he had helped to set England on the way to becoming the mistress of the seas.

EXPLORATION DATES

1513	1521
1498	1493
1497	

JOHN CABOT
(1450?–99?)

VASCO NÚÑEZ DE BALBOA
(1475–1519)

HENRY HUDSON
(1565?–1611)

FERDINAND MAGELLAN
(1480?–1521)

SIR WALTER RALEIGH

Birthplace: Devonshire, England

Born: 1554?

Died: 1618

In 1595 Raleigh led an expedition to what is now Venezuela, in South America, sailing up the Orinoco River in the heart of Spain's colonial empire. He described the expedition in his book *The Discoverie of Guiana* (1596).

ALL THE WORLD'S A STAGE

A drama, or play, is basically a story acted out. Every play—whether it is serious or humorous, ancient or modern—tells its story through characters in situations that imitate human life. A play's author is called a dramatist or playwright. The playwright's characters must be vivid, interesting, and, most important, different enough from each other so that their actions somehow create a conflict or predicament. This conflict underlies another important element of a play: its plot—that is, what happens and why.

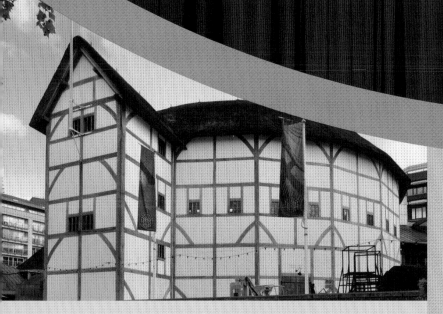

The Globe Theatre, a famous London, England, theater in which after 1599 the plays of William Shakespeare were performed

KNOW YOUR SHAKESPEARE!

The Tempest

Romeo and Juliet

Twelfth Night

A Midsummer Night's Dream

Titus Andronicus

WILLIAM SHAKESPEARE

Birthplace: Stratford-upon-Avon, England

Born: 1564

Died: 1616

For more than 350 years, William Shakespeare has been the world's most popular playwright. His plays are filled with action, his characters are believable, and his language is thrilling to hear or read. Underlying all this is Shakespeare's deep humanity. He was a profound student of people and he understood them. He had a great tolerance, sympathy, and love for all people, good or evil.

HENRIK IBSEN

Birthplace: Skien, Norway

Born: 1828

Died: 1906

The first great modern playwright was Henrik Ibsen, a Norwegian. His plays show a wide variety of styles, ranging from the realism of *Hedda Gabler* to the fantasy of *Peer Gynt*. He is admired for his technical mastery, symbolism, and deep psychological insight.

ANTON CHEKHOV

Birthplace: Taganrog, Russia

Born: 1860

Died: 1904

The stories and plays written by Anton Chekhov describe in almost sociological detail the Russian society of his day. However, modern readers value his works chiefly for their deep insight into human emotion. Such is his subtlety that it is often difficult to decide whether a particular work is a comedy or a tragedy.

GEORGE BERNARD SHAW

Birthplace: Dublin, Ireland

Born: 1856

Died: 1950

George Bernard Shaw's first play, *Widowers' Houses*, was performed in 1892. It was the first of many plays, nearly all successful. His main purpose as a dramatist was to shock people out of conventional, hidebound ways of thinking. His view of his work was reflected in the title of his collection *Plays: Pleasant and Unpleasant*, published in 1898.

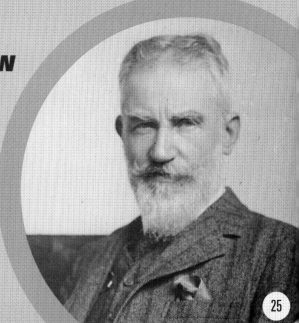

BRILLIANT BREAKTHROUGHS

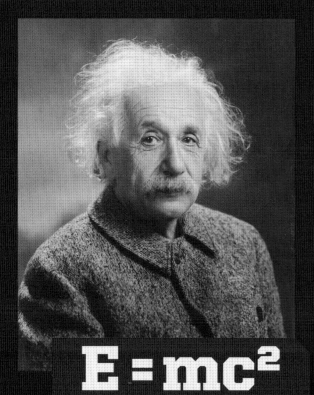

$$E = mc^2$$

ALBERT EINSTEIN

Birthplace: Ulm, Germany

Born: 1879

Died: 1955

In 1916 Albert Einstein published his general theory of relativity. In it he proposed that gravity is not a force, a previously accepted theory, but a curved field in the space-time continuum that is created by the presence of mass.

Worldwide fame came to Einstein in 1919 when the Royal Society of London announced that predictions made in his general theory of relativity had been confirmed. He was awarded the Nobel Prize for Physics two years later; however, the prize was for his work in theoretical physics, not relativity theories, which were still considered to be controversial.

CHARLES DARWIN

Birthplace: Shrewsbury, England

Born: 1809

Died: 1882

ON

THE ORIGIN OF SPECIES

BY MEANS OF NATURAL SELECTION,

OR THE

PRESERVATION OF FAVOURED RACES IN THE STRUGGLE
FOR LIFE.

BY CHARLES DARWIN, M.A.,

**NIELS BOHR
(1885–1962)**

**MAX PLANCK
(1858–1947)**

**NIKOLA TESLA
(1856–1943)**

MOMENTS OF GENIUS

James Clerk Maxwell (1831–79)

Heinrich Hertz (1857–94)

Ernest Rutherford (1871–1937)

Guglielmo Marconi (1874–1937)

Alfred Wegener (1880–1930)

MARIE CURIE

Birthplace: Warsaw, Poland
Born: 1867
Died: 1934

Marie Curie is the only woman in history to have won the Nobel Prize in two different fields. In 1898 she and her husband, Pierre, announced their discovery of radium and polonium. In 1903 they shared the Nobel Prize for Physics with Henri Becquerel.

After Pierre died in 1906, Marie carried on their research. She also became the first woman professor at the Sorbonne. In 1911 she won the Nobel Prize for Chemistry for isolating pure radium.

OTTO HAHN

Birthplace: Frankfurt am Main, Germany
Born: 1879
Died: 1968

Chemist Otto Hahn is credited, along with radiochemist Fritz Strassmann, with discovering nuclear fission. This development led directly to the creation of atomic weapons during World War II and to the modern nuclear power industry. Hahn was awarded the Nobel Prize for Chemistry in 1944.

EDWIN POWELL HUBBLE

Birthplace: Marshfield, Missouri
Born: 1889
Died: 1953

Generally regarded as the leading astronomer of the 20th century, Edwin Powell Hubble made discoveries that convinced the great majority of astronomers that the universe in fact contains many galaxies. In studying those galaxies in the late 1920s, Hubble made his second remarkable discovery: that the galaxies were receding from the Milky Way at rates that increased with distance. This implied that the universe, long considered unchanging, was expanding.

Science plays a major role in society, and even nonscientists can appreciate scientific progress. Because of science, human understanding of the past, present, and future is constantly in a state of flux.

ENRICO FERMI

Birthplace: Rome, Italy
Born: 1901
Died: 1954

On December 2, 1942, the first man-made and self-sustaining nuclear chain reaction was achieved, resulting in the controlled release of nuclear energy. This feat took place in a squash court beneath the stands of an unused football stadium at the University of Chicago in Illinois. The scientist who led the achievement was Enrico Fermi. The first practical use of the ability to control nuclear energy was in the atom bombs that were used at the end of World War II.

WERNER HEISENBERG

Birthplace: Würzburg, Germany
Born: 1901
Died: 1976

For his work on quantum mechanics, the German physicist Werner Heisenberg received the Nobel Prize for Physics in 1932. He will probably be best remembered, however, for developing the uncertainty (or indeterminacy) principle, the concept that the behavior of subatomic particles can be predicted only on the basis of probability. Isaac Newton's laws of motion, therefore, cannot be used to predict accurately the behavior of single subatomic particles.

ERWIN SCHRÖDINGER

Birthplace: Vienna, Austria
Born: 1887
Died: 1961

The Austrian theoretical physicist Erwin Schrödinger contributed to the wave theory of matter and to other fundamentals of quantum mechanics. For new forms of atomic theory he shared the 1933 Nobel Prize for Physics with the British physicist P.A.M. Dirac.

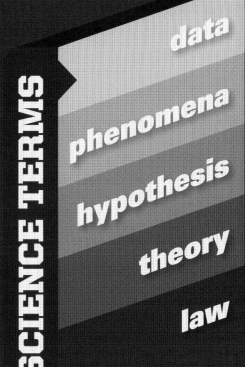

SCIENCE TERMS

data

phenomena

hypothesis

theory

law

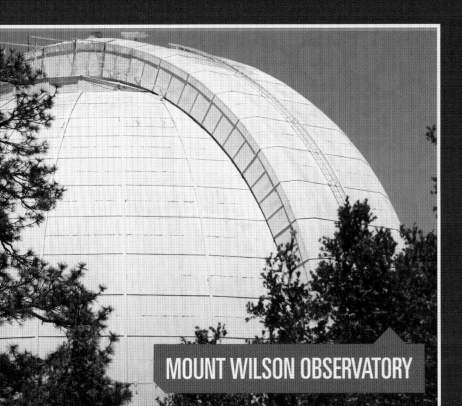

MOUNT WILSON OBSERVATORY

MEDICAL MAESTROS

The practice of medicine—the science and art of preventing, alleviating, and curing disease—is one of the oldest professional callings. Since ancient times, healers with varying degrees of knowledge and skills have sought to restore the health or relieve the distress of the sick and injured.

The ancient Greek doctor Hippocrates is considered the Father of Western Medicine. He treated medicine as a science. He made detailed observations of his patients and thought that diseases had a physical cause.

WILLIAM HARVEY

Birthplace: Folkestone, Kent, England
Born: 1578
Died: 1657

MAESTRO MATCH

THE HIPPOCRATIC OATH

Hippocrates is best known today for his ethical code (Hippocratic Oath), which continues to be used by the medical profession as a guide to appropriate conduct. The oath is a pledge doctors make to always use their knowledge and best judgment for the benefit of their patients and to never harm or injure those in their care.

ALEXANDER FLEMING

Birthplace: Lochfield, Ayrshire, Scotland
Born: 1881
Died: 1955

LOUIS PASTEUR

Birthplace: Dole, France

Born: 1822

Died: 1895

From Pasteur to Pasteurization

The French chemist Louis Pasteur showed that heat killed the microbes that cause fermentation. This discovery led to his invention of a process for destroying harmful microbes in food. This process became known as pasteurization. It slows down the spoiling of food. Pasteurization is still used today.

WILHELM ROENTGEN

Birthplace: Lennep, Prussia

Born: 1845

Died: 1923

Recipient of the first Nobel Prize for Physics in 1901, German physicist Wilhelm Roentgen is the discoverer of X rays. His achievement heralded the age of modern physics and transformed medical practice.

FREDERICK GOWLAND HOPKINS

Birthplace: Eastbourne, East Sussex, England

Born: 1861

Died: 1947

The British biochemist Frederick Gowland Hopkins received (with Christiaan Eijkman) the 1929 Nobel Prize for Physiology or Medicine for discovery of essential nutrient factors—now known as vitamins—needed in animal diets to maintain health.

ROENTGEN'S X RAYS

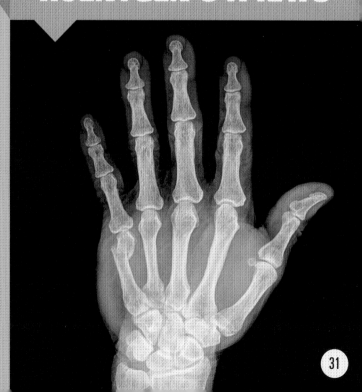

MEDICAL
FACT OR FICTION?

FACT | FICTION

VICTORIAN NOVELISTS

FICTION OR BIOGRAPHY?

| CHARLES DICKENS | DICKENS CHARACTER |

CHARLES DICKENS

Birthplace: Portsmouth, Hampshire, England
Born: 1812
Died: 1870

Key works: *Oliver Twist* (1838), *A Christmas Carol* (1843), *David Copperfield* (1850), *A Tale of Two Cities* (1859), *Great Expectations* (1861)

Charles Dickens was praised in his lifetime, and his critical reputation has only grown since his death. He is generally considered the greatest writer of the Victorian era, and some critics place him second only to William Shakespeare in all of English literature.

WILLIAM MAKEPEACE THACKERAY

Birthplace: Calcutta, India
Born: 1811
Died: 1863

Although his popularity began to decline at the end of the 19th century, William Makepeace Thackeray in his own time was regarded as the only possible rival to Charles Dickens. Thackeray's *Vanity Fair* (1847-48) is the first novel in English to show a woman who is neither very good nor very bad but only very human. His *The History of Pendennis* (1848-50) is the story of an all-too-human man. In *The History of Henry Esmond, Esq.* (1852) Thackeray blended fact and fiction into a believable historical novel; in *The Newcomes* (1853-55) he used his own knowledge of the social world of England and India.

JANE AUSTEN

Birthplace: Steventon, Hampshire, England
Born: 1775
Died: 1817

Key works: *Sense and Sensibility* (1811), *Pride and Prejudice* (1813), *Mansfield Park* (1814), *Emma* (1815)

Through her portrayals of ordinary people in everyday life Jane Austen gave the genre of the novel its modern character. She wrote of the world she knew. Her novels portray the lives of the gentry and clergy of rural England, and they take place in the country villages and neighborhoods, with an occasional visit to Bath and London. Her world was small, but she saw it clearly and portrayed it with wit and detachment.

THOMAS HARDY

Birthplace: Higher Bockhampton, Dorset, England
Born: 1840
Died: 1928

Key works: *Under the Greenwood Tree* (1872), *Far from the Madding Crowd* (1874), *The Return of the Native* (1878), *Tess of the d'Urbervilles* (1891)

The continuing popularity of Thomas Hardy's novels owes much to their richly varied yet always accessible style and their combination of romantic plots with convincingly presented characters. Equally important—particularly in terms of their suitability to film and television adaptation—is their nostalgic evocation of a vanished rural world through the creation of highly particularized regional settings.

ANTHONY TROLLOPE

Birthplace: London, England
Born: 1815
Died: 1882

Key works: The *Chronicles of Barsetshire* are Trollope's best-known books. They include *The Warden* (1855), *Barchester Towers* (1857), *Doctor Thorne* (1858), *Framley Parsonage* (1861), *The Small House at Allington* (1864), and *The Last Chronicle of Barset* (1867)

Anthony Trollope also wrote convincing novels of political life as well as studies that show great psychological penetration. One of his greatest strengths was a steady, consistent vision of the social structures of Victorian England, which he re-created in his books with unusual solidity.

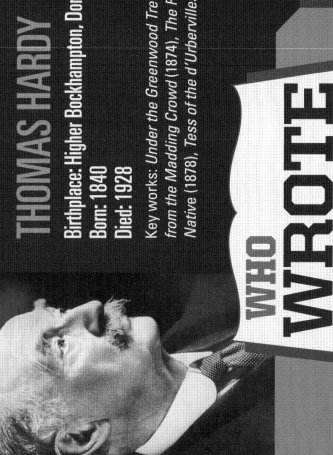

WHO WROTE THAT?

THE BRONTË FAMILY

The bleak, lonely moors of Yorkshire in England were the setting for two great novels of the 19th century. These were Charlotte Brontë's *Jane Eyre* and Emily Brontë's *Wuthering Heights*, which were both published in 1847. Readers today are still enthralled by their tragic, romantic stories and by the sense of brooding mystery that shrouds the tales. The youngest sister, Anne, was also a talented novelist, and her books have the same haunting quality.

AMERICAN POETS

T.S. ELIOT

BIRTHPLACE: ST. LOUIS, MISSOURI
BORN: 1888
DIED: 1965

In 1915 the verse magazine *Poetry* published T.S. Eliot's first notable piece, *The Love Song of J. Alfred Prufrock*. It is considered to be the first masterpiece of modernism in English. In this poem and others collected in *Prufrock and Other Observations* (1917), Eliot tried to create new verse rhythms based on the rhythms of contemporary speech. In 1919 he published a second collection, *Poems*. Eliot won international acclaim with the appearance of *The Waste Land* in 1922.

ROBERT FROST

BIRTHPLACE: SAN FRANCISCO, CALIFORNIA
BORN: 1874
DIED: 1963

Although Robert Frost sold his first poem in 1894, he was not able to earn a living as a poet until more than 20 years later. His honors include Pulitzer prizes in 1924 for *New Hampshire* (1923), in 1931 for *Collected Poems* (1930), in 1937 for *A Further Range* (1936), and in 1943 for *A Witness Tree* (1942). Among his other books were *Mountain Interval* (1916), *West-Running Brook* (1928), and *In the Clearing* (1962).

E.E. CUMMINGS

BIRTHPLACE: CAMBRIDGE, MASSACHUSETTS
BORN: 1894
DIED: 1962

E.E. Cummings's first book of verse was *Tulips and Chimneys* (1923). In all he wrote 12 volumes of verse, which were collected in *Complete Poems* (1968). The strangeness of his style was criticized by some as phony and pretentious, but others found it meaningful despite the difficulties it often posed.

EARLY POETS

HENRY WADSWORTH LONGFELLOW
(1807–82)

EMILY DICKINSON
(1830–86)

WALT WHITMAN
(1819–92)

EDGAR ALLAN POE
(1809–49)

20TH-CENTURY MODERNISTS

EZRA POUND
(1885–1972)

WALLACE STEVENS
(1879–1955)

WILLIAM CARLOS WILLIAMS
(1883–1963)

MARIANNE MOORE
(1887–1972)

FAMOUS LINES

Once upon a midnight dreary, while I pondered, weak and weary,

He says again, 'Good fences make good neighbors.'

(with up so floating many bells down)

The apparition of these faces in the crowd;

When the evening is spread out against the sky

SET IN STONE

By the simplest definition, architecture is the design of buildings, executed by architects. However, it is more. It is the expression of thought in building. It is not simply construction, the piling of stones or the spanning of spaces with steel girders. It is the intelligent creation of forms and spaces that in themselves express an idea.

CHRISTOPHER WREN

Birthplace: East Knoyle, Wiltshire, England
Born: 1632
Died: 1723

St. Paul's famous dome has long dominated the skyline of London, England. Wren's cathedral was completed in 1710.

FRANK LLOYD WRIGHT

Birthplace: Richland Center, Wisconsin
Born: 1867
Died: 1959

Taliesin

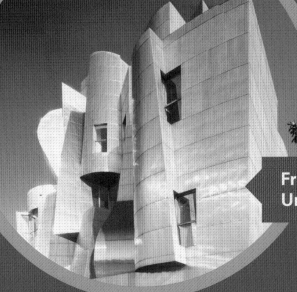

FRANK O. GEHRY

Birthplace: Toronto, Canada
Born: 1929

Frederick R. Weisman Art Museum at the University of Minnesota in Minneapolis

NAME THAT ARCHITECT

ANTONI GAUDÍ I CORNET

Birthplace: Reus, Spain
Born: 1852
Died: 1926

One of the first sites to be visited by tourists in Barcelona, Spain, is the Sagrada Família, or Church of the Holy Family. The building, as yet unfinished, was the lifework of architect Antoni Gaudí.

WHO BUILT THE PARTHENON?

Located on the Acropolis, the Parthenon is the largest Doric temple on the Greek mainland. According to the inscription on the building, the construction was begun in 447 BC.

THREE COMPOSERS OF NOTE

JOHANN SEBASTIAN BACH

Birthplace: Eisenach, Thuringia (Germany)

Born: 1685

Died: 1750

Johann Sebastian Bach created hundreds of musical compositions, including works for choir, orchestra, and individual instruments, especially the organ. Many of these were for use in churches or in instruction. His works brought to a climax the Baroque period, during which many new forms and styles were developed.

WOLFGANG AMADEUS MOZART

Birthplace: Salzburg, Austria

Born: 1756

Died: 1791

Wolfgang Amadeus Mozart is often considered the greatest musical genius of all time. His output—especially in view of his short life—was enormous, including multiple operas, symphonies, piano and five violin concerti, string quartets, masses, and other works in every form popular in his time.

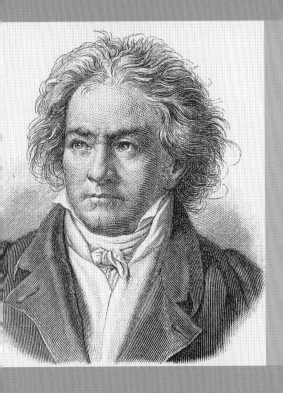

LUDWIG VAN BEETHOVEN

Birthplace: Bonn, Germany

Born: 1770

Died: 1827

Ludwig van Beethoven's music was unique and emotional. Never before had instrumental music, which had previously been considered inferior to vocal music, been brought to such heights. He also made great strides with chamber music for piano, as well as for string quartets, trios, and sonatas. His works include symphonies, piano sonatas, piano concerti, string quartets, a violin concerto, sonatas for violin and piano, an opera (*Fidelio*), the *Mass in C Major*, and the mass known as *Missa Solemnis*.

TEN KEY COMPOSERS

FRANZ SCHUBERT
(1797–1828)

GEORGE FRIDERIC HANDEL
(1685–1759)

ANTONIO VIVALDI
(1678–1741)

CLAUDE DEBUSSY
(1862–1918)

JOHANNES BRAHMS
(1833–97)

JOSEPH HAYDN
(1732–1809)

FRÉDÉRIC CHOPIN
(1810–49)

IGOR STRAVINSKY
(1882–1971)

GIUSEPPE VERDI
(1813–1901)

PYOTR ILYICH TCHAIKOVSKY
(1840–93)

IN MUSICAL TERMS

fugue

opera

oratorio

symphony

concerto

THOUGHTS WITH IMPACT

JEAN-JACQUES ROUSSEAU

Birthplace: Geneva, Switzerland

Born: 1712

Died: 1778

Major works: *Discourse on the Origin of Inequality* (1755), *The Social Contract* (1762)

ROUSSEAU'S INFLUENCE ON:

GOVERNMENT

EDUCATION

LITERATURE

HENRY DAVID THOREAU

Birthplace: Concord, Massachusetts

Born: 1817

Died: 1862

Major works: "Civil Disobedience" (1849), *Walden* (1854)

THOREAU'S "CIVIL DISOBEDIENCE"

NICCOLÒ MACHIAVELLI

Birthplace: Florence, Italy
Born: 1469
Died: 1527

Major works: *The Prince* (written 1513, published 1532), *Discourses on Livy* (written beginning in 1513, published 1531)

MACHIAVELLI'S *THE PRINCE*

MARX'S THE COMMUNIST MANIFESTO

KARL MARX

Birthplace: Trier, Rhine province, Prussia (Germany)
Born: 1818
Died: 1883

Major works: *The Communist Manifesto* (1848), *Das Kapital* (1867)

WORKS THAT CHANGED THE WORLD

THOREAU'S *WALDEN*

WALDEN POND

THE MIND'S INNER WORKINGS

Psychology is the scientific study of the ways that people think, feel, and behave. Like anthropology and sociology, psychology is called a social science. Scientists trained in psychology are called psychologists. Psychologists study the human mind and emotions to try to understand the reasons behind people's actions.

SIGMUND FREUD

BIRTHPLACE: **FREIBERG, MORAVIA, AUSTRIAN EMPIRE (NOW PRÍBOR, CZECH REPUBLIC)**
BORN: **1856**
DIED: **1939**

Important publications: *The Interpretation of Dreams* (1899), *The Psychopathology of Everyday Life* (1904)

Freud's creation of **psychoanalysis** was at once a theory of the human psyche, a therapy for the relief of its ills, and an optic for the interpretation of culture and society.

JUNG OR FREUD?

JUNG   FREUD

CARL JUNG

BIRTHPLACE: **KESSWIL, SWITZERLAND**
BORN: **1875**
DIED: **1961**

Important publications: *Psychology of the Unconscious* (1916), *Psychological Types* (1923)

Jung proposed and developed the concepts of the extraverted and the introverted personality, archetypes, and the collective unconscious.

ALFRED ADLER'S INDIVIDUAL PSYCHOLOGY

BIRTHPLACE: **PENZING, AUSTRIA**

BORN: **1870**

DIED: **1937**

Important publications:
The Neurotic Constitution (1912),
Understanding Human Nature (1927)

B.F. SKINNER: BEHAVIORISM

BIRTHPLACE: **SUSQUEHANNA, PENNSYLVANIA**

BORN: **1904**

DIED: **1990**

Important publications:
The Behavior of Organisms (1938), *Science and Human Behavior* (1953), *Beyond Freedom and Dignity* (1971)

IVAN PAVLOV

BIRTHPLACE: **RYAZAN, RUSSIA**

BORN: **1849**

DIED: **1936**

From 1890 to 1900 Pavlov analyzed the secretory activity of digestion in animals. Through his observations Pavlov was able to formulate the laws of conditioned reflex. This subject occupied much of his time until 1930. After 1930 he began to apply his laws to the study of the human mental illnesses called neuroses and psychoses.

PSYCHOLOGY'S FOUNDER: WILHELM WUNDT

An ink blot, similar to those used in the Rorschach test, is designed to elicit a description that is used by the tester to gain insight into the personality of an individual.

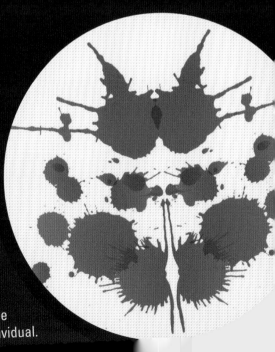

FIVE FOUNDING FATHERS

On February 4, 1789, George Washington was unanimously elected president of the United States. His presidency was to be a time of adjustment to a new type of government for the people of the United States. Washington believed in a strong federal, or central, government. He also believed that the United States should remain neutral in foreign affairs. Political parties developed because of his views. The Federalists, such as Alexander Hamilton, supported Washington's ideas. The Democratic-Republicans, such as Thomas Jefferson, defended the power of the states. Washington tried to keep a balance between the two parties.

Another problem faced by Washington was finding ways to pay the expenses of the new government. Congress passed taxes on certain products, including whiskey. In 1794 farmers in Pennsylvania rebelled against the whiskey tax, prompting Washington to send about 13,000 soldiers to end the rebellion. His actions showed the power of the federal government.

	Washington begins his military career in the French and Indian War.		Great Britain surrenders.		Washington becomes the first U.S. president.		Federal troops suppress the Whiskey Rebellion.		Washington dies at Mount Vernon.
1732	1754	1775	1781	1787	1789	1793	1794	1797	1799
Washington is born in Westmoreland County, Va.		Washington leads the Continental Army into the American Revolution.		Washington heads the Constitutional Convention.		Washington issues the Proclamation of Neutrality.		Washington retires to Mount Vernon.	

In 1800 Thomas Jefferson and Aaron Burr ran for president against President John Adams. Jefferson and Burr received the same number of electoral votes. The House of Representatives eventually chose Jefferson as the winner.

The most important event of Jefferson's first term was the purchase of a large area of land known as the Louisiana Territory from France in 1803. The territory doubled the size of the United States. The president launched the Lewis and Clark Expedition to explore the new territory. Jefferson easily won reelection in 1804, but his second term was less successful than the first. A war between Britain and France hurt U.S. trade with Europe.

	Jefferson writes the Declaration of Independence.		Jefferson succeeds Benjamin Franklin as U.S. minister to France.		Jefferson is elected vice president under President John Adams.		The Louisiana Purchase doubles the size of the United States.		Jefferson dies at his home near Charlottesville, Va.
1743	1776	1779	1785	1789	1796	1800	1803	1809	1826
Jefferson is born in Shadwell, Va.		Jefferson becomes the governor of Virginia.		President George Washington makes Jefferson his secretary of state.		Jefferson is elected president.		Jefferson retires after a second term.	

JAMES MADISON
(1751–1836)

JAMES MADISON: FATHER OF THE CONSTITUTION

James Madison drafted a large portion of the Constitution based on his principles of a strong national government and an even distribution of authority within its branches. His dedication to these values and his diligent participation in the convention earned him the title Father of the Constitution.

JOHN ADAMS AND THE CONTINENTAL CONGRESS

In 1774 colonists in Massachusetts elected John Adams to the Continental Congress. There he asked George Washington to serve as commander of the Continental Army, the military force of the colonies during the American Revolution. He also chose Thomas Jefferson to write the Declaration of Independence.

NOTABLE FIRSTS

JOHN ADAMS
(1735–1826)

ALEXANDER HAMILTON
(1755?–1804)

ALEXANDER HAMILTON AS SECRETARY OF THE TREASURY

George Washington chose Alexander Hamilton to be the first secretary of the treasury. It was in this office that he did most to shape the struggling young government. Hamilton's financial measures assured payment of the foreign and domestic debts of the United States. Under his leadership the federal government also took over the debts contracted by the separate states as a result of the American Revolution. Hamilton gained congressional support for this provision by agreeing to locate the federal capital in the South on the Potomac River. Hamilton restored the credit of the United States—his greatest achievement. He also established a national bank.

AMERICAN INGENUITY

ELI WHITNEY

BIRTHPLACE: **WESTBORO, MASSACHUSETTS**

BORN: **1765**
DIED: **1825**

Eli Whitney designed machine tools by which an unskilled workman made only a particular part that conformed precisely to a model. The sum of such parts was a musket. Any part would fit any musket of that design. He had grasped the concept of interchangeable parts. "The tools which I contemplate to make," he explained, "are similar to an engraving on copper plate from which may be taken a great number of impressions perceptibly alike."

THOMAS EDISON

BIRTHPLACE: **MILAN, OHIO**

BORN: **1847**
DIED: **1931**

From Thomas Edison's laboratories and workshops came the phonograph, the carbon-button transmitter for the telephone speaker and microphone, the incandescent lamp, a revolutionary generator of unprecedented efficiency, the first commercial electric railroad, and key elements of motion-picture apparatus, as well as a host of other inventions.

Diagram of Whitney's cotton gin

Wilbur and Orville Wright putting their plane on a launching rail in 1909

ALEXANDER GRAHAM BELL

BIRTHPLACE: EDINBURGH, SCOTLAND
BORN: 1847
DIED: 1922

On Alexander Graham Bell's first successful test of the telephone, he spoke a few words, beginning with "Mr. Watson, come here." After his success with the telephone, Bell pursued his interests in science, invention, and the education of deaf people.

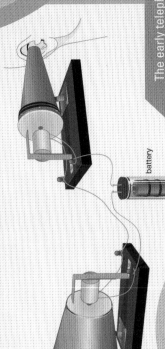

battery

The early telephone looked very different from the telephones we use today.

INGENIOUS INVENTIONS

1794	1877
1888	1900
1908	

In 1896 Henry Ford built his first car in a small shed behind his home. It had a gasoline-powered engine, four bicycle tires attached to a buggy frame, a steering lever instead of a wheel, and a single seat. In 1903, the Ford Motor Company was founded.

Cyrus McCormick, an American industrialist and inventor, is generally credited with the development (from 1831) of the mechanical reaper.

47

HISTORY'S MOST
HORRIBLE

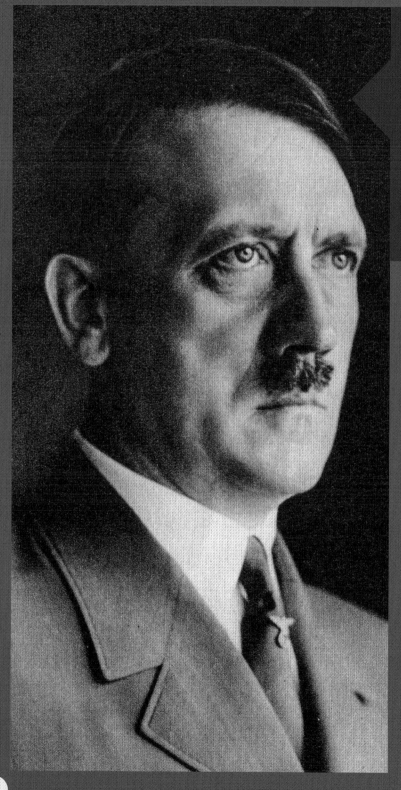

ADOLF HITLER
(1889–1945)

The rise of Adolf Hitler to the position of dictator of Germany is the story of a frenzied ambition that plunged the world into the worst war in history. Only an army corporal in World War I, Hitler became Germany's chancellor 15 years later. By 1934 he had obtained full power and adopted the title *Fuhrer*, or "leader."

HITLER'S IMPACT

- THE NAZI PARTY
- BEER HALL PUTSCH
- WORLD WAR II
- THE HOLOCAUST

FASCISM

One of the major forms of government of the 20th century is called fascism. Fascism, along with communism (and to some extent, socialism), holds to the notion that the state is supreme over the individual. It is therefore the responsibility of all individuals to work together for the betterment of the state.

Fascism forges a political alliance with capitalism, working with those who control production, for the better economic functioning of the nation. It exalts the nation (or, as in Germany, the nation and race) as the supreme value, and it uses the police and military powers of the state to enforce its policies.

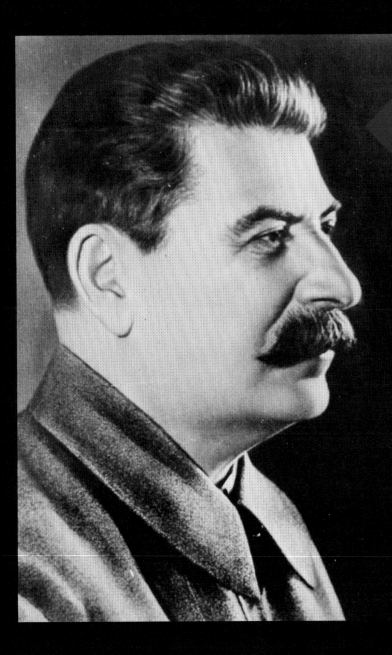

JOSEPH STALIN
(1879–1953)

One of the most ruthless dictators of modern times was Joseph Stalin, the despot who transformed the Soviet Union into a major world power. The victims of his campaigns of political terror included some of his followers. His original Georgian name was Ioseb Dzhugashvili. In 1912 he took the alias of "Stalin," from the Russian word *stal*, meaning "steel."

STALIN'S IMPACT

- THE BOLSHEVIKS
- THE GREAT PURGES
- WORLD WAR II

TOTALITARIANISM

It is the "total" in totalitarianism that gives the best clue to its meaning. The term refers to the type of government that attempts to assert total control over the lives of its citizens. This form of tyranny was a 20th-century development that was instituted to serve the goal of transforming society according to socialist principles. Totalitarian governments first appeared shortly after World War I. They lasted in various places for about 70 years before proving to be political and economic failures.

It was Benito Mussolini, dictator of Italy from 1922 to 1943, who coined the word *totalitario* to describe the goals of his fascist government. He explained the term by saying that his aim was "All within the state, none outside the state, none against the state."

HORRIBLE ENDS

FIVE NOTORIOUS DICTATORS

A dictatorship is a form of government in which one person or a small group possesses absolute power. Dictators usually resort to force or fraud to gain despotic political power; they remain in power through the use of intimidation, terror, and the suppression of basic civil liberties. They may also employ techniques of mass propaganda in order to sustain their public support.

- **BENITO MUSSOLINI** (1883–1945)
- **KIM IL-SUNG** (1912–94)
- **IDI AMIN** (1924/25–2003)
- **POL POT** (1925–98)
- **SADDAM HUSSEIN** (1937–2006)

MOHANDAS KARAMCHAND GANDHI

Birthplace: Porbandar, India
Born: 1869
Died: 1948
Gandhi was a leader of India's independence movement. When India was a colony of Great Britain, Gandhi used nonviolent methods to protest against British rule. His efforts earned him the title Mahatma, which means "great soul."

PROTESTS IN INDIA

INDEPENDENCE

CIVIL DISOBEDIENCE

Civil disobedience is a symbolic, but nevertheless real, violation of what is considered an unjust law rather than the rejection of a whole system of laws and government.

Gandhi read Henry David Thoreau's "Civil Disobedience" and formulated his doctrine of nonviolent resistance to the British colonial authorities. It was also among the texts that inspired Martin Luther King, Jr., the leading proponent of nonviolent resistance in the United States.

GREAT HUMANITARIANS

A humanitarian is a person devoted to or working for the health and happiness of other people.

FLORENCE NIGHTINGALE (1820–1910)	HENRI DUNANT (1828–1910)
MOTHER TERESA (1910–97)	HELEN KELLER (1880–1968)
HARRIET TUBMAN (c. 1820–1913)	NORMAN BORLAUG (1914–2009)

MARTIN LUTHER KING, JR.

Birthplace: Atlanta, Georgia
Born: 1929
Died: 1968

While helping grassroots leaders mobilize African Americans for sustained mass struggles, Martin Luther King, Jr., inspired participants to believe that their cause was just and consistent with traditional American values of equality. He also appealed to the consciences of all Americans, thus building popular support for civil rights reform. His strategy of emphasizing nonviolent protest and interracial cooperation enabled him to fight effectively against the Southern system of legalized racial segregation and discrimination; however, the method proved inadequate during his final years as he sought to overcome racial and economic problems that were national in scope.

WHO SAID IT?

PRIZEWINNING HUMANITARIANS

- NOBEL PRIZE FOR PEACE
- JEWEL OF INDIA
- ORDER OF MERIT
- POPE JOHN XXIII PEACE PRIZE
- PRESIDENTIAL MEDAL OF FREEDOM

REVOLUTION

The word revolution means "turning around." Politically, a revolution is a rapid transformation of society. It is typically a violent alteration in government and in related associations and structures.

VLADIMIR ILICH LENIN

Birthplace: Simbirsk, Russia
Born: 1870
Died: 1924

Few individuals in modern history had as profound an effect on their times or evoked as much heated debate as the Russian revolutionary Vladimir Ilich Lenin. To his supporters, Lenin appeared as the individual who, through the sheer force of his will and dedication to the revolutionary struggle, played the decisive role in the Russian Revolution of 1917 that brought about the first government dedicated to overturning the political and economic system of Western capitalism. His detractors denounced Lenin as an antidemocratic despot who, through the use of bloody repression and indiscriminate terror, laid the foundation for the first modern totalitarian police state.

SIMÓN BOLÍVAR

Birthplace: Caracas, Venezuela
Born: 1783
Died: 1830

Simón Bolívar led revolutions against Spanish rule in South America. The countries of Venezuela, Colombia, Ecuador, Panama, Peru, and Bolivia all owe their independence largely to him.

REVOLUTIONARY DATES

1920 1953 1921
1949 1917

BIOGRAPHICAL

MAO ZEDONG

Birthplace: Shaoshan, Hunan Province, China

Born: 1893

Died: 1976

Mao Zedong was a Chinese Marxist theorist, soldier, and statesman who led his country's communist revolution. When China emerged from a half century of revolution as the world's most populous nation and launched itself on a path of economic development and social change, Mao occupied a critical place in the story of the country's resurgence. Looking at the whole period from the foundation of the Chinese Communist Party in 1921 to Mao's death in 1976, many scholars regard Mao as the principal architect of the new China.

Birthplace: Southeastern Cuba

Born: 1926

In January 1959 Fidel Castro's force of 800 guerrillas defeated the Cuban government's 30,000-man professional army. As the undisputed revolutionary leader, Castro became commander in chief of the armed forces. In February 1959 he became premier and thus head of the government.

Castro's early attempts to instigate Marxist revolutions elsewhere in Latin America foundered. However, Cuban troops did eventually serve as proxies for the Soviet Union in various conflicts in less-developed countries.

WHAT IS GUERRILLA WARFARE?

EMILIANO ZAPATA

Birthplace: Anenecuilco, Mexico

Born: 1879

Died: 1919

In 1910 Emiliano Zapata was involved with the political struggle in Mexico to end the dictatorship of President Porfirio Díaz and to prompt land reform. By 1911 the revolutionary troops had forced Díaz from power. Fighting continued, however, and in November 1914 Zapata's 25,000-man Liberation Army of the South occupied Mexico City. Two weeks later Zapata formed an alliance with revolutionary Pancho Villa to work together for a civilian president. Zapata created a commission to distribute land and established a Rural Loan Bank, Mexico's first farm credit organization. On April 10, 1919, Zapata was ambushed and shot to death.

THE GREAT AMERICAN NOVELIST

The middle of the 19th century saw the beginning of a truly independent American literature. This period, especially the years 1850–55, has been called the American Renaissance. More masterpieces were written at this time than in any other equal span of years in American history.

NATHANIEL HAWTHORNE

Nathaniel Hawthorne (1804–64) was a master of the allegorical and symbolic tale. One of the greatest fiction writers in American literature, he is best known for *The Scarlet Letter* (1850) and *The House of the Seven Gables* (1851). Hawthorne's work initiated the most durable tradition in American fiction, that of the symbolic romance that assumes the universality of guilt and explores the complexities and ambiguities of man's choices.

WHO WROTE IT ❓

FIRST TO FAME

James Fenimore Cooper (1789–1851) was the first American novelist to achieve worldwide fame. Robert Louis Stevenson called him "Cooper of the wood and wave," because he wrote about American Indians and pioneers in the forest and sailors on the high seas. In 1823 Cooper wrote *The Pioneers*, the first of five Leatherstocking Tales. They include *The Last of the Mohicans* (1826), *The Prairie* (1827), *The Pathfinder* (1840), and *The Deerslayer* (1841).

HERMAN MELVILLE

Herman Melville (1819–91) used his adventures in Polynesia as the basis of his first successful novels, *Typee* (1846) and *Omoo* (1847). Melville developed a complex, highly individual writing style using richly symbolic language. Largely neglected during his lifetime, he is now regarded as one of the greatest of American writers.

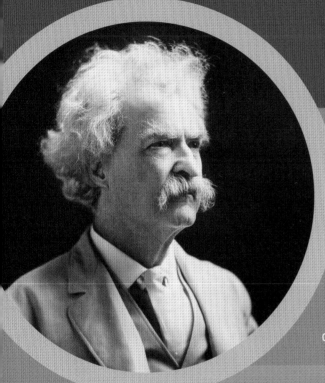

MARK TWAIN

A onetime printer and Mississippi River boat pilot, Mark Twain (1835–1910) became one of America's greatest authors. His *Tom Sawyer* (1876), *Life on the Mississippi* (1883), and *Huckleberry Finn* (1884) rank high on any list of great American books.

The controversial *Huckleberry Finn*, which is periodically banned in schools or libraries because of alleged racial overtones, can be read by children, but it is not a child's book. It has elements of heartbreak and wisdom that can be appreciated best by adults. On the other hand, *Tom Sawyer* is primarily a juvenile book, but adults can also enjoy it.

BIOGRAPHICAL BITS

HARRIET BEECHER STOWE

Harriet Beecher Stowe (1811–96) wrote *Uncle Tom's Cabin* based on her reading of abolitionist literature and on her personal observations in Ohio and Kentucky. The book was an immediate sensation and was taken up eagerly by abolitionists while, along with its author, it was vehemently denounced in the South, where reading or possessing the book became an extremely dangerous enterprise. With sales of 300,000 in the first year, the book exerted an influence equaled by few other novels in history, helping to solidify both pro- and antislavery sentiment.

THE FIRST PERSON TO...

NEIL ARMSTRONG

BIRTHPLACE: **WAPAKONETA, OHIO**
BORN: **1930**
DIED: **2012**

The first person to set foot on the Moon was U.S. astronaut Neil Armstrong. As he stepped onto the Moon's dusty surface, he spoke the now famous words, "That's one small step for [a] man, one giant leap for mankind."

BY THE NUMBERS

13   33.5   18
4.75   12

CHARLES LINDBERGH

BIRTHPLACE: **DETROIT, MICHIGAN**
BORN: **1902**
DIED: **1974**

On May 20–21, 1927, Charles Lindbergh flew a small silvery monoplane, called the *Spirit of St. Louis*, nonstop from New York City, New York, to Paris, France. It was the first one-man flight across the Atlantic Ocean. The daring, skill, and endurance of "Lucky Lindy" won him world acclaim. After his flight Lindbergh devoted his career to aviation and science.

YURY GAGARIN

BIRTHPLACE: WEST OF MOSCOW, RUSSIA
BORN: 1934
DIED: 1968

The world's first astronaut was a 27-year-old Soviet aviator named Yury Gagarin. On April 12, 1961, the spacecraft Vostok 1 was launched at 9:07 in the morning, Moscow time. The spacecraft orbited the Earth once in 1 hour and 29 minutes at a maximum speed of 17,000 miles (27,000 kilometers) per hour. It followed an elliptical orbit that carried Gagarin as far as 187 miles (301 kilometers) from Earth.

CHUCK YEAGER

BIRTHPLACE: MYRA, WEST VIRGINIA
BORN: 1923

In 1947 Chuck Yeager was chosen to test-fly the experimental X-1 aircraft. The rocket-engined X-1 was designed to determine if a straight-wing plane could fly faster than the speed of sound. There was also the question of whether a pilot could successfully control the plane despite the battering effects of shock waves. On October 14, 1947, over Rogers Dry Lake in California, Yeager rode the X-1—attached to the belly of its B-29 mother ship—to an altitude of 25,000 feet (7,600 meters). He then released the aircraft from the B-29 and rocketed to an altitude of 40,000 feet (12,200 meters). Flying 662 miles (1,065 kilometers) per hour with the X-1 intact, Yeager became the first person to break the sound barrier.

ALEKSEY ARKHIPOVICH LEONOV

BIRTHPLACE: LISTVYANKA, NEAR KEMEROVO, RUSSIA
BORN: 1934

On March 18, 1965, Voskhod 2 was launched into space with Aleksey Arkhipovich Leonov and Pavel Belyayev aboard. During the second orbit Leonov let himself out of the spacecraft by means of an air lock while about 110 miles (177 kilometers) above Crimea. Tethered to the ship, Leonov made observations, took motion pictures, and practiced maneuvering in free-fall for about 10 minutes before reentering the ship. It landed after completing 17 orbits (26 hours) in space.

MAKING THE FUTURE REAL

BILL GATES

BIRTHPLACE: SEATTLE, WASHINGTON
BORN: 1955

Bill Gates started tinkering with computers early, writing software from the age of 13 and helping to computerize his high school's payroll system. He formed Microsoft with childhood friend Paul G. Allen. Microsoft began its domination of the fledgling microcomputer industry when Gates licensed the operating system MS-DOS to IBM in 1980 for use in IBM's first personal computer. Microsoft quickly became the leader in the huge, fast-growing personal computer market. By 1986 Gates was a billionaire.

REAL OR NOT?

REAL	NOT

ELON MUSK

BIRTHPLACE: PRETORIA, SOUTH AFRICA
BORN: 1971

In 2002 Elon Musk founded Space Exploration Technologies (SpaceX) to make more affordable rockets. Its first two rockets were designed to cost much less than competing rockets. SpaceX also developed the Dragon spacecraft, which carries supplies to the International Space Station and is designed to carry as many as seven astronauts. Musk sought to reduce the expense of spaceflight by developing a fully reusable rocket that could lift off and return to the pad it launched from. Beginning in 2012, SpaceX's Grasshopper rocket made several short flights to test such technology.

STEVE JOBS

BIRTHPLACE: SAN FRANCISCO, CALIFORNIA
BORN: 1955
DIED: 2011

After developing the Apple I computer in 1976, entrepreneurs Steve Jobs and Steve Wozniak found themselves at the forefront of an industry on the verge of an explosion. Their fledgling enterprise, Apple Computer, Inc., quickly set the standard for personal computers and made the duo millionaires while still in their 20s.

TIM BERNERS-LEE

BIRTHPLACE: LONDON, ENGLAND
BORN: 1955

In 1989 Tim Berners-Lee drew up a proposal for creating a global hypertext document system that would make use of the Internet. His goal was to provide researchers with the ability to share results without having to exchange e-mail constantly. Instead, researchers would place such information "online," where peers could immediately retrieve it anytime. Berners-Lee wrote the software for the first Web server and the first Web client between October 1990 and the summer of 1991.

VISIONARIES THAT MADE TODAY POSSIBLE

- Arthur C. Clarke (1917–2008)
- R. Buckminster Fuller (1895–1983)
- Carl Sagan (1934–96)
- Robert Noyce (1927–90)

SEARCH ENGINE FOUNDERS

Larry Page 🔍

and

Sergey Brin 🔍

MILESTONES

IN WHICH CITY DID SOCRATES LIVE AND TEACH?

SPARTA

ATHENS

WHICH ARTIST PAINTED THE CEILING OF THE SISTINE CHAPEL?

LEONARDO DA VINCI

MICHELANGELO

THE BOOK TITLE OF HENRY DAVID THOREAU'S EXPERIMENT IN BASIC LIVING WAS CALLED:

THE PRINCE

WALDEN

DISCOVERED IN 1928, THIS SUBSTANCE IS NOW USED TO FIGHT VARIOUS INFECTIONS.

LYSOZYME

PENICILLIN

WHO INVENTED THE ALTERNATING-CURRENT POWER SYSTEM THAT PROVIDES ELECTRICITY FOR HOMES AND BUILDINGS?

NIKOLA TESLA

THOMAS EDISON

WHOSE TELESCOPE OBSERVATIONS VERIFIED THAT THE UNIVERSE IS EXPANDING?

EDWIN POWELL HUBBLE

GALILEO GALILEI

WHO WAS THE FIRST ENGLISHMAN TO SAIL AROUND THE WORLD?

SIR WALTER RALEIGH

SIR FRANCIS DRAKE

WHICH OF THE FOLLOWING WAS ONE OF THOMAS EDISON'S INVENTIONS?

FIVE-NEEDLE TELEGRAPH

TINFOIL PHONOGRAPH

CYRUS MCCORMICK MADE THE LIVES OF FARMWORKERS EASIER BY INVENTING THIS.

MECHANICAL COW MILKER

MECHANICAL GRAIN REAPER